Standing Watch

The Houghton Mifflin New Poetry Series

Standing Watch

CHRISTOPHER BURSK

HOUGHTON MIFFLIN COMPANY   BOSTON 1978

Library of Congress Cataloging in Publication Data

Bursk, Christopher.
    Standing watch.

    (Houghton Mifflin new poetry series)
    I. Title.
PS3552.U765S7   811'.5'4   78-13288
ISBN 0-395-27118-5

Printed in the United States of America

V 10 9 8 7 6 5 4 3 2 1

Magazines in which the following poems previously ap-
peared are: *Attention Please* (Hearthstone Press): "Victory
March." *Beloit Poetry Journal*: "Adjust, Adjust," "April
9, 1945 / Bewahrung," "Town Beach," "When Are You
Going to Grow Up?" *Hiram Poetry Review*: "Bedtime,"
"Knowing I Would Lose Her Again." *Images*: "Two of
Your Great-Aunt's Dreams." *Paris Review*: "Gravity,"
"Thieves, Arabs of the Tall Grass." *Poetry Now*: "Family
Reunion," "Recess," "Root Darkness." *The Sun*: "At the
Mouth of the Cave," "Companions," "Long Before Hark-
ness's Father Shot Himself There" (under the title "Look,
Look"), "Namesake," "Silence" (under the title "Passenger
Seat"). *The Windless Orchard*: "Infidelities." *Xanadu*:
"The Year Grandmother — Father's Mother — Came to
Run the Household." *Hyacinths and Biscuits*: "Aviary"
(under the title "Refuge").

For Catherine Irwin Bursk and Edward Collins Bursk,
for Mary Ann Adzarito Bursk,
for Pamela Perkins Atkinson,
for Christian, Norabeth, and Justin

Contents

Standing Watch

Family Reunion

You are afraid of swimming,
do not like anything to lift and lull you
till you drift buoyant
and swift as it — afraid of horses as well and cautious of men,
they are a pleasure to touch,
to walk beside.
You would have the sea beside you like a husband
you could satisfy with your hands,
you could watch fall out of your hands into sleep.

Your son is afraid of water; at sea's edge he knows
his bones will survive him,
his skin will drop away like an old man's pajamas.
He is naked enough to know he is bones alive.
You have told him of his soul, one day he will dive,
swim out of it, kick if off
like loose trunks. He is skinny,
watching himself
picked up, studied, memorized by the waves.

His grandmother is afraid of the current. She knows
how a few waves carry it in
like well-wishers covering their mouths,
bearing in enough of disease.
She remembers black curtains in neighbors' windows,
smallpox wagons.
She is afraid for herself, seventy-two, at the beach,
nylons rolled to the ankles,
never having swum the sea she had to cross.

Her son is afraid of the currents too.
He makes love as if remembering a sorrow
in his wife's childhood. He dreams of being swept to sea
calling to her, to his sons.
They are asleep and do not stir. Waves stall
like rescue boats around him.
He shrieks over their dimming lights, "Who will kiss you goodnight?
Who will check the burners and try the locks?
Who will turn out the lights?"

I am his brother, the one he tried to teach to swim
at Government Island, the one in the orange life jacket,
the one in the photo he is trying to push
off the dock's edge. I clung to the swimming ladders,
saw how deep down one could climb.
"Jump! Jump!" the other boys shouted
as if I were suicide enough to be a man,
fool enough to try.

The Year Grandmother – Father's Mother – Came to Run the Household

I

"Those are the only cookies you get.
If you want cookies, young man, you must eat this kind."
The rest of the house was dark
except for the long hall
and the pantry. The house smelled of 'scotch-lace cookies
and an old woman's perfume.
The cookies were as delicate as doilies,
they broke in my hands.

II

My father and I are playing dolls.
We are the dolls,
sitting at the wrong end of the bed
trying to be quieter
than our bodies. We have the good ears
of dolls, the sharp hearing
of bodies that wait to be lifted.
We are not touching.
Dolls don't.

The Sitting

He would wake in the daybed to the scratching
of knife and thumbnail on canvas.
There was always a white space: an old friend's hand
or the hem of a dress or a jonquil
his mother would not consent to,
one corner she had to scrape white again.

Her fingers were blue and pink from sunsets
she had rubbed off skies.
She would rub the skin off his father's face,
raise his cheekbones
and darken his cheeks
till his father disappeared.

Her fingers smelled of linseed and turpentine.
They tipped the boy's chin,
pressed along his cheeks
till he felt the skin slide over his jaws — Why, he was only a skull —
and he thought of the cat's skull
he had cupped like a bird's nest.

His mother made him sit for hours
while she erased his bones.
He tried not to move, to look as sadly beautiful
as the face she kept making vanish,
kept trying to work the light into,
to work light into her oils.

When he began finding her crying on curbstones,
he decided to be sick enough to stay home
and pose in the sunroom. He dozed off
listening to her press light into the canvas
till her brushes splayed, her knife failed her
and he woke to find her painting with her fingers.

He was afraid to come home and find alizarins
and cadmiums scrubbed off the handles of coffee cups,
burnt siennas off curtains, zinc white off the dining-room table,
and another hired woman smiling like a mother
in a coloring book, the house full of yellow flowers,
everything faithful and copied.

Better to be home in the sunroom sick,
painter and model
and portrait, one white space still left to be shadowed in,
his mother talking to the light again,
evening flattening his fleshtones as he tried not to move
out of the little light left her.

Knowing I Would Lose Her Again

I lay beside my mother in a dark room
that floated on sunlight, loosening its moorings
from the rest of the house,
lilting in the sunlight that tilted our windows
lifting us like high tides lifting docks
as we lay on them.

I thought of my father listing below,
our house swamping, brothers
drowning in the submerged parts of the house,
only this sunlight surrounding my mother's room
like the calmed surfaces
after a great ship has mysteriously gone down.

I remember lying there, knowing how years from then
I would have to dive for brothers,
would have to let some thick and ugly man's body
like the huge weight of a divingsuit
be drawn over me,
breathe his hair, be fastened inside his damp skin.

I would have to go down for all the brothers I let drown,
organs jostled, settling
like things crammed into suitcases,
water packed thick around me,
knowing then, going down,
how little I could change in my life,

How when I rose, when I tried to live
I would have to wade air,
part it with strokes close to my body
as if trying to run in water.
I lay beside my mother in a dark room
lifted by sunlight, rocking

In sunlight that leaked in at cracks
in the blinds, hands bailing,
cupping warm water,
pouring sunlight over myself
and over my mother,
knowing I would lose her again.

Root Darkness

There was another darkness, the snake's
and the forsythia's: root darkness. His mother said
it was what flowed through their flat rakes,
what splashed their spades,
the high-water rim of the dark earth rising
and left for good on their shovel blades,
shadows left on stones that had been underground
longer than the boy had lived.
Darkness made him feel he had never lived,
as if he were a small possibility,
a word waiting to be spoken,
curled microfilm, a seed.

He felt like a seed in a seed's trance.
What would his father think of him, dreamy as clematis
floating off trellises? as seeds clinging
to each other like girls waiting to be asked to dance?
He crouched in the dark, earning his allowance,
wringing the necks of sheep sorrel
and chickweed, reaching for weeds
as if he were reaching into someone's throat
and drawing out the veins.
There was no darkness to his father, only a dusk
that smelled of wallets, smoking jackets, evening trains,
of light kept to a schedule.

He used to imagine his father could force the light
before its time, cut it back to the crown
of its roots, bury it outside.

It was his father who opened the windows,
sun leafing through the blinds
like chicory or endive through the slats in a basket.
No one had ever died that the boy could remember;
his father kept everything alive.
Earth meant nothing to the boy but darkness.
What were their bodies but darkness,
pods of darkness that had not yet broken open.

His mother leaned over the porch rail, watching her garden
as if she had just set it down by the handle
into darkness, breathing in deep the bitter teas
of turned-over peat moss. She liked to say
she was letting her garden steep.
The darkness was hers, he knew the darkness by her.
She pressed his hands down into the earth
till he dared dig out new growth when he wrenched out old.
"Your father hates to get his hands dirty."
She rubbed the boy's hands with soil, forced them
into the dirt. They weeded silently together,
left old roots to rot. The earth dried gray
on his fingers. In bed
he could still feel the dark earth rising to meet him.

Thieves, Arabs of the Tall Grass

for Herb Fredericks

The winds smell of thieves' markets, of sweetbreads,
of rinds candied with thick syrups of the sun, of trees
glistening like dark men rubbed with oil.

In the dusk after school we are no one's sons, Arabs of the tall grass.
Caravans of trees cross our trails,
yellows, scarlets flapping like sleeves of many great robes.

Even the winds do not suspect the shadows we cast
in the back alleys of woods
where we murder each other effortlessly.

We lead small children into the dark
and leave them crying. The dark can be merciless,
we learn to be as unkind.

We follow winds like streets in a city before the birth of Christ,
come upon houses like travelers
to lights of inns, we have no need to go farther.

Loved, we have no need for love;
thieves, surprised in other people's houses, we wait for night,
we touch our bodies like jewels made of paste.

In the tall grass each of us watches for his father
to stride home with trophies like Orion.
We tag after him like the Dog Star at his heel.

Long Before Harkness's Father
Shot Himself There

for my brother, 1938–1971

Father warned us to stay away from the barn,
queer town character
whose face leaned to one side,
whose snow fences sagged
like argyll socks around the ankles,
slow child we threw stones at
till everything we could break was broken.

I recall only the dumb mooning face
of a car that has crashed
and this barn
through whose cracked slats in the root cellar
years earlier we crawled, whispering each other's names.
We crouched after hands
we raised before our faces

Afraid to reach into the troughs of darkness,
to run our hands over the sweaty shanks
of beasts more tremendous
than any ever stabled,
to steal among this shadowy livestock
as if their troubled thighs
would sway and crush us.

Darkness hung over us like sides of beef.
You made me listen for sounds of animals
being slaughtered, for the man

with the hammer to swell out of the dusky blood
and stumble forward,
lift his smeared apron over us.
You shrieked, "Look, look!"

And made me follow you up ladders,
curled my fingers around the few good rungs,
picked cobwebs and insect wings off my sleeves.
I stiffened till I felt the damp spaces
between my body and my clothes
and you made me look down

Four flights down,
made me watch you swing out over the chute,
your nine-year-old arms barely touching both sides,
your body sinking
almost bearing you down
as you hung there,
crying, "Look, look!"

Victory March

The war over,
his mother's letters put away, each week, in a shoebox
like a child's first homework,

What does the boy remember of that year
besides learning the way to every old woman in town?

He remembers lining up,
he remembers the war was over
because the teachers cut crepe paper
and taped it to the children,
stuffed it into their sleeves and down their collars:

Each of the first four grades
a garden vegetable, head of lettuce, stalk of celery,
carrot, tomato, radish.

He does not remember which he was,
only that it felt good
to be outside and marching through cemeteries,
crepe paper crinkling and stretching,
it felt good to let strips of paper ripple over his lips,
to blow them away,
to dampen them with his tongue.

He has forgotten the cooing of other children's mothers,
smirking and pointing older kids,

teachers' voices triggered
exploding behind him like mines.

He remembers only the forbidden mild tastes
of paper softening
and darkening on his lips.

April 9, 1945 / Bewahrung

From my house I was sure I could hear everything in the world.
I could tell the channel buoys
like the bells of different churches,
could hear the sea mumbling its low mass, hurrying the gospel,
mending the same dark clothing
it had been saving the poor for years.
I could hear each wave arrive late, slide into its pew,
tell each piece of change
dropping into the collection plate.

From my house I could hear everything — if I was quiet
I could tell between churches
like old boats in the harbor. I had closed my eyes so often
I knew whose hulls took the waves
like doors closing in empty factories, hulls of which fleet
rattled like windows shut all through a house.
I heard each church drift to tether's end
and pull at its slack — from my house I heard churches creak
as they were tugged back.

From my house I could hear everything — if I did not move
I could hear everything else that did not move,
dark buildings groaning like wharves,
roofs I clung to
looking down, watching myself fall — I could tell the buildings
by how far they had sunk down,
which was Harvard, which mother's hospital;
from my house I heard waves rise over its wards,
every day heard my mother drown.

From my house I was sure I heard everything else in the world,
all the countries shifting at their moorings.
Eyes closed, I could hear Germany move
among them like a freighter in too small a harbor.
I knew its cargo by its wake,
heard millions of small stones being scraped back.
From my house I heard the waves rise again
like bordering countries,
heard their feudal, cresting, holocaustal surf break.

Catch

This is how you throw a ball
when you are alone

when you are alone
you have somebody else's hands

you take the throw on one bounce;
this is how you play at ten

staring at your belt,
shaking off signals

the slow windup of old relievers, looping flowery *J*s and *L*s
painstaking signatures to each pitch

you brush the batter back,
you feel the burn marks on your cheeks

at ten throwing hard, one hand playing
the other.

Morning Papers

You had to dress in the kitchen,
to beat the train and everybody else's father to town,
to wait on the stone step-up
and listen to empty trains (hollow
as wastebaskets, as houses
before anyone wakes up and you knock something over
and try to stop the noise
from having happened)
and cut wire off the morning papers.

You had to learn again how silence let you speak
to all that was silent: your bike,
other boys' dogs, the Georgian houses
of blind women who tipped you two cents each week,
houses of girls who made up sing-song about you,
boys who beat you up.
You had to learn how much the town was yours, its damp streets
drying like towels on the line overnight.

You had to be the one to speak the first words
spoken in town that day,
to pedal conversations through your head,
long talks you would finally have with your father,
scores you would play to sudden death
(you loved the long driveways
you could finish a whole murder in). You learned to be wet
and let your clothes dry on you

To cover Korea under your jacket and read
about the Brinks robbery
or Joe McCarthy over one hedge and under another,
to change your clothes, read cereal packages,
take out Mark Trail wildlife cards
from between the shredded wheat, then put on your safety
patrol badge and bike to school.
This is the only thing you are proud of.

Recess

Older boys drag younger by the wrists into woods,
children letting themselves go heavy,
letting themselves sink down inside their shirts.

My son backs against the walls
as if he were watching a brush fire spread toward him,
child by child; he looks away.

In half-empty subways I try not to gaze at coveys of thin boys
touching their hair as if it were on fire,
slicking down the flames.

Boys cursing, blowing smoke in our faces
as if they wanted us to rise
so they could set something else on fire.

As a child I knew I would always be afraid.
My son knows, I see it in his eyes,
in his soft, helpless hands after school.

I hear him in the white light before morning, in his terrible
and unsupervised recesses,
pressed to the wall, crying uncle, uncle.

Hands

Because it possesses both strength and lightness of touch
the hand is wonderfully adaptable to all sorts of uses.
— *Compton's Encyclopedia*

The boy's fingers are Simon, John,
brother James, doubting Thomas
and good fat Thaddeus, the faithful Judas

fishermen and tax collectors,
his left hand

the one closest to his body,
the one that touches

Little Simon, sorcerer,
the one always at the edge, about to step out of the picture
and go back to his spells of wasp venom and rat whiskers,
to conjuring coins out of hair;
showoff, smart aleck, pip-squeak, the cute one, the apostle's pet,
street cur fiercely loyal once won over,
the finger that never fits into a prayer
and skitters at the mouth of a cave
like a spooked bat.

On either side of Thomas, John
and silent James,
the middle brother, bashful, athletic,
a third wheel,
the one looking away while the others touch,
the reliable one, team player,
the one that lines up,
that blocks head-on.

His brother John,
the unmarried one, the poker, the pusher,
the one at sales conventions
and stag parties, the one who votes a straight ticket,
who passes orders on down,
ward heeler, hero worshipper, statistician,
loudmouth, lifelong friend
who takes the shit.

Doubting Thomas, the boy's favorite, tall, quiet, sober,
the oldest,
the one the others huddle next to,
the closest one, the first to touch the skin.

And fat Thaddeus, Squire Busybody,
hospital administrator,
Little League umpire,
the happy drunk at the other end of the bar,
the one who orders a round for the house.

Not a suicide
not a betrayer among them

his left hand

The boy looks at his knuckles till they smile
cracked idiotic smiles,
weary kind smiles,
his fingers are always about to break into their old hymns
like country preachers,
itinerants,
they are always mouthing an odd and tender gospel.

He has learned to talk to his hands so softly
no one turns to look.

This is my bad hand, he tells his father,
his right hand:

Saul, Simon Peter, two others who only nod,
Bartholomew and Andrew, advance men,
gofers, quick as sparrows; Saint Paul smells like a principal,
someone who has taken enough courses
and has seniority,
who wears white socks, whose voice reaches down the hall.

And there is one more finger,
the one on whose nail he draws a face and erases it,
the one the boy makes stories for
and becomes: peevish, easily offended, aloof, passionate,
always testing another's love,
the one who has to touch the bead of rain on a leaf
and rub it out, who tries to trap a snowflake
and keep it on its tip until it melts,

The other Judas.

Silence

Outside a hundred visiting Indian scholars sang to you,
mother's soprano lifting over theirs
like someone in a choir who forgets
and lets her voice surge before the others.
Even the hired help carrying away pots of saltwater
and stoneware of shells
joined in as if singing for a child of their own.

Mother made us say the names of businesses you had saved,
say out loud the names of cities
you were traveling to. This is how we learned geography.
She peeled apples by the fire,
her voice rising with anger and love, "Your father is like God,
I don't want you boys ever to forget that."
Her words reached into the unlit parts of the house.

You would be gone for days.
We used your furniture instead of you,
curling in whatever made a lap for us.
We took turns crawling into your bed
scratching the finish off the headboard,
its softened patina wadding under our nails like sunlight
that had been caking there for years.

I hated you for the shynesses I caused you
as I heard you belt yourself back
into the darkness on the other side of the car.
We rode from Boston to Cape Cod, every night,
listening to each other's hands.

I could hear the breaths you swallowed back
seconds before you spoke
like someone trying to get the courage to dive.

Father, I always thought you were waiting
for me to begin, for me to say the words
that would let you love me.
Even at four I knew if I were to touch you
I would hurt you more than you could bear.
At thirteen I knew if I were to rest my hand on your leg
or let it graze the stubble of your cheek

We would swerve terribly, be flung out of our seats
sick and afraid, the space between us
dissolving, its sugars
clouding the cold clear waters of the poles.
We would drown, breaking through ice
like brothers trying to save each other,
borne down by each other's weight,
drowning in each other's arms.

Playing Little

Saturday, lording over loneliness,
lifting lead soldiers out of long, flat boxes,
he closes his hands around bodies
he has worn smooth, lifted ridges of pants,
lilt of legs, tuck of thighs, detailed nakedness
of Indians, muscles rippling across muscles
like waves crossing waves.

He examines faces till he believes them again
till the film leaves their eyes
and they wake like small predators half-dead from winter sleep.
He scratches them till the lead shows through
like bone, till they flinch
and he becomes as small as they, tastes the dull solder
of another's body, feels himself poured
into their casings, burned back to hard detail,
glazed and fired for the final time.

It is better to be theirs, to mold machine guns and gas masks
to them, fix them to green slits of land
they must defend, gunfighters —
wiry sullen boys trapped in the draw, trigger fingers
unable to tremble — wounded confederates
raising their faces shyly
like girls being kissed for the first time.
Assassins creep into his pockets,
crawl into the folds of his pants legs,
slide deep into his sleeves;
ambassadors arrive in the high, dark court of his lap

smelling of licorice.
He lets himself be tortured and teased,
it feels like warm water being poured on his back, his legs

Till he grows cold on the sunroom floor,
feels the numbed spaces between boards, between windows,
other rooms remote as drugged nerves
he reaches across great distances to touch,
to touch again, each time expecting
feeling to spurt back.
He shivers, moves back into his own body,
upstairs lets others have him,
yielding to larger hands than his own.

Sexes

Ovenbird, jenny wren, titmouse
snow bunting, white throated sparrow,
waxwing, warbler,
thimbles and spools, buttonholes
and apronpockets.
Little women

Goshawk, Gyrfalcon,
Raven, Turkey Vulture,
Crow, Grebe, Grackle,
the way a name
is spoken, hard
unshakable fact, names
heavy to the hand
like a hammer, grip
of a wrench, birds
fashioned like good tools
to last

As a boy he sorted everything into sexes,
into species

pinfish
threadfish
butterfish
silver perch
nursehound

Flounder
Stargazer
Cutlass
Pigfish
Wrymouth

summer flies, fleas, gnats
sounds of threads
being pulled through,
snarls combed out of long hair

Wasp, Hornet
razorstrop, hairbrush;
with his father
he held his breath
as if watching a wasp walk
    up his arm,
the back
of his father's hand

magnified
sudden dark pores
like the blown-up
pictures of insects

Touching a man
is like touching
a snake
in a museum (they say
it won't hurt him,
the boy knows better):

dull comfortable reptiles,
turtles, tortoises,
their names
like the names of plain women

Coral Snake, Cottonmouth,
Scarlet King Snake,
Diamondback, Coachwhip,
Texas Blind Snake,
Sand Boa, Python

He used to lie in bed and divide the weather into sexes:

Spring, someone's daughter
in the drugstore
leafing through movie magazines

Summer, fat, unwashed farmer
in town,
picking up young girls

Fall, bitter woman drinking alone
at her kitchen table

Winter, silent man
who uses his silence
to dull others into obedience
his dray horses
dragging huge, flat sleds
across a soil
it has taken years to build

Handyman

He was blue black and safe as the cellar,
his hands smelled of ashes, claypots, roots, piperust, wrenches.
He put his hands over mine
and brought down hammers,
he let me go down and feed the burners and curse the pipes
as if I alone kept the house afloat.

Father descended, highborn, expendable,
giving orders;
we let him monkey with the controls,
but it was the hired man and I who kept everything from dying.
All August we fastened black hoses
we kept patched and clear of shrubs.

Where the hired man was, it was cool as toolsheds, as old tools.
Afternoons I pulled my wagon after him
filled with hedge clippings, briars, tools.
I learned to let my cuts stay dirty and heal black,
to stand in one place and rake small piles around me,
to make each task move around me,

To work without moving like the hired man.
Alonso moved so slowly
he could never hurt, never be hurt
working under father's sedan or mother's sink.
I loved to be allowed to take things down to him,
one bottle, one tall glass on a tray

Listen to him sip ale beside the garage door
and tell of the daughter he'd left in the West Indies,
Look out at naptime and see Alonso wheeling his barrow in,
his old dog lying across my father's dead flowers
too old to bite anyone,
too old to do anything but follow behind Alonso's bike.

Anyone who rode a bicycle was safe, was not a father,
was harmless as overalls, as fat bicycle tires.
Alonso was always leaning over boys,
moving their hands, teaching them to wash windows, stoke coal,
mow his grass,
we always spoke of the grass as Alonso's.

When he died, I had to rake the grass my brother mowed.
I let the grass fall lightly, puffed it up,
made pockets of air in the cuttings. Paid by the basket,
I wanted to earn my pay honestly but easily like the hired man,
to stretch out the lawn as Alonso had
and make the grass last.

Aviary

Encella, ensajai
encantas sunta challdor

I knew if I spoke these words
someone listened.
                    Not you,
                    words for you were: Sorry
                                No thank you, sir
                                I don't know
                                May I

Encantas sunta challdor, antanti
braslsis, tonsjon,
xhalla, xhalla
(a small aviary of sounds, birds
whose names only I knew
and tried to keep still as branches for

hoverings
body feathers, stiff mesh of long-flight feathers,
blind reptilian fury,
wings beating
like the arms of a child, sobbing, thrashing
out of someone older's arms)
                                If you would only try
                                Please try
                                Just this once
                                Speak, damnit
                                For your own sake, try

Taskunto
Noscatti unsunja, unsunja tasji ensajai
Sattar, noscati sunta

"Over two thousand strong, beetlecats swarm over waters from Cohasset, Mass., to Babylon, L.I."

— F. S. Blanchard, *The Sailboat Classes of North America*

Sneakboxes, dabchicks, daysailers
swarm over waters like summer flies,
like tiny black bugs that scuff the pools at low tide.
I begged my brothers not to take me out of sight of land.
If I could see the town clock, I was safe.

Wedged in between the rocks, the beach looked like an old shoe.
We were proud of our history of shipwrecks,
read aloud to the school assemblies poems about drowning
        immigrants.
Our people found them,
my brothers told me no one in town ever drowned.

In Cohasset a boy got to be a man by capsizing
and learning to shed his pants in the water.
A boy grew up boat by boat: Scorpion, Moth, Mercury, 110, 210.
Adolescence was genoa jibs and spinnakers,
old age centerboard and mainsail again.

By fifteen my brothers were polishing long sleek mahogany boats,
fine furniture that would last.
They bought them with their own money
and lived as if in bachelor pads,
rode in cockpits two by two.

I manned the stopwatch, they let me crew
as they fumbled with the soft blouses of spinnakers,
reaching before Bemis and Bowditch, men who ran their 210s

with as shrewd a sense of winds as of corporations,
trimming jibs, tacking on a bonanza of breezes.

I liked to sail inside the harbor with the old marrieds
waving from the sideseats of Herreshoffs
they had varnished dark and glossy as 1940s beach wagons.
I hoped for winds too heavy even for my brothers.
Our boat heeled like a small company going under,

Like our father, years later, the business gone bad,
still luffing others to windward.
I had to hike, swing out on the trapeze, hold our boat down.
I was brought along for extra weight,
younger brothers were good for ballast,

Good for pulling boats back into moorings.
They pushed me over. After all that time on the sea
It was good to sink into it, feel my pants fill with water,
let go my piss, feel it warm my skin,
feel the old pleasures of surrender, tread water, swim in.

Tongues and Slugs

That summer, worrying thoughts of our fathers
like loose teeth, we had the same teasing pleasures,
the same dread of waking, gagging
on small, hard ivory fragments.
Our dreams were obscene, impertinent
as tongues. Our tongues had another life,
they lived like slugs
culling and scraping. In captivity, one book says,
a slug accepted dead mice, toilet soap, sea holly.
"The great gray slugs invade dairies
to sip the cream
of which they are so desperately fond."
After our fathers were gone,
our tongues fretted open cankers, oblivious
as slugs that feast like amnesiacs.
At thirteen we were always ravenous
wanting to fill that hollowness
we felt in us like a grave
not shoveled in.
We filled our pockets with moon snails,
slipper shells, baby's ears.
We gouged out the white tongues
of mollusks, made shells babble to us
like drunken uncles.
I dreamed I curled my legs back over me,
my feet lipped over me
like the foot of a snail, body drawn forward
till I could touch the tip
of my penis, and I woke

as always from dreams, groggy and gluttonous.
This is what I could not tell you,
fatherless and famished,
this is what we shall never speak of,
we who are fathers. Twenty years later
I learn the names and habits
of all those things I never dared touch.
I read of the large black slug,
how it will often eat the slime off the back
of another. Though this is certain death,
the victim stands still
as if he were indifferent to such business
that gives the other pleasure.

Other Rooms

In most houses there is a room a child will not enter,
a drawer he will not pull out
when anyone is home. Every child has one old woman
he is guiltily afraid of,
whose kisses he cannot forget.
In every neighborhood there is a larger boy.
Every boy has a place,
somewhere between home and somewhere else:
sag in a fence, dry belly of a puddle, curbstone where he widens
cracks other boys have opened.
Every boy has one street he looks for from the window
of a train or bus and wonders
what it would be like to buy a soda in the dark small cornerstore,
to sip it on one high stone step
of the rowhouse and watch the train
leave. Every boy has a place
where he wishes he had said yes,
a city street just late enough to make everyone else
look older, a guest room
at a friend of his father's, men's room in a terminal.
A place he longs for afterward,
its padded old men bent over,
scrimmaging, practicing blocks
between benches like second stringers,
pants slipping off them like hip pads, voices slurred
as if through mouth guards,
they mumble scores of games or names of girls
like secret places where they hid
as children, lean over him, old runaway fathers

puzzling out the new math
of his body. Every boy has one young man he remembers
who touched him
and he felt himself tilting
as if trying to stand in a small boat,
one young man who spoke German,
whose fingernails smelled of smoke. There is always one room
he is sorry he never entered.

False Bride

The birch pulls bones out of its long white woman's throat.
Spring comes to town like the circus,
tents pitched, rigging hoisted, a fanfare of jonquils,
a freakshow,
flowers sweated like sugar crystals out of a clenched fist,
an old woman unhatched
still living off her yolk.

The princess,
that fairytale daughter of her father's dotage,
that well-sucked pacifier,
an only child, is sent to smooth things over,
to be given in marriage,
to be dropped in the turnstile like a subway token.

Serving women help to pack her jewels,
her silver spoons.
(You listen. Why are you here?
Two weeks ago I lifted you from under a car.)

The queen takes a sharp knife,
lets three drops of blood fall upon her handkerchief,
tucks this in her daughter's bosom. (You

want to turn the page.)
Surely he would not let her bleed for long,
she would long for home,
the prince would smile like a girl,

they would tell stories on fathers,
how their organs grew bloated and drunk
as feudal lords.

"Please turn down my sheets,
please get down and fetch water in my golden cup,
comb the road out of my hair,
fan me until I grow drowsy and can dream of swans."
The serving girl strips her mistress,
makes her promise never to tell.
She sends her to tend geese. (You lean against me
staring at the silver silhouettes
of their naked bodies. You look deep into the crimson darkness
of lakes, the bleeding dyes of a fairytale woods.

Have you been here before? You gaze
at the flicking pages
as if watching from a train.)

Evening after evening
the princess tells her story to the ashes,
sifts through cinders for an earring, a brooch,
sobs with the spellbound self-pity of the high born
as if their sorrow could save them
and death would grow ashamed of his base intentions,
his rough laborer's hands.

(All these years I have pretended
it matters; being molested
is a cheap terror, getting off the train and running;
he placed a jeweled knife next to me.
"Use it. If you don't trust me,
use it." He rubbed his fingers over me
as around the smudged rims of waterglasses on counters.
The stone subway platforms stretched

like unforgivingly dull passages in the Bible,
station after station
like verses to be learned.)

"What doom does such a false bride deserve?"
the king asks, having listened
to cinders, their small mouths gossiping
idle in the flames.
The serving maid suspects nothing on her wedding day,
replies, "Put her stark naked in a barrel
stuck with nails, drag her by two white horses through the streets."
(The queer sentence themselves

to death. I was thirteen. Doctors were lit for me like banquet halls.

This is not my child I ease out from under the car,
begging, "Don't close your eyes."
I pick up the doll, it's not even broken; my cries
hover like innocent bystanders, hands
over mouths.

I wait for a fate equal to my birth.
You grow weak in my arms.
I am thinking of something else.)

Adjust, Adjust

I was born committing suicide
holding my breath, they had to drag me kicking
out of that damp garage, airtight inside,
gases I struggled back to
until the doctor slapped me alive
and shouted, Survive, survive.

After Hiroshima, turning four,
I battered my head at the master bedroom door.
Every night I dreamt I was a child
burning at the town dump at the world's edge, Japan;
and every night my father yelled, Be brave.
Behave, behave.

I ripped his set of Plato at eight,
the year my mother was put away at Boston State,
and war was fought in a darkness called Korea;
all winter I played dead in the corner
while my teachers clapped,
Adapt, adapt.

Grandmother took me in till I was ten;
with her silver carving knife I locked her with me
in the den, all night clinging to her bathrobe, demanding
we cut our wrists in a lovers' pact.
The only answer I could secure
was, Endure, endure.

I counted my bones, waiting to be dead,
at thirteen an invalid in my nursing home, my bed,
watching Arkansas homemakers rail at Negro girls
between commercials, first graders
whom they tried to storm,
shrieking, Nigger, nigger, conform.

At fifteen, in South Station where I ran away every week,
I bedded down on papers inksmudged with the blood
of freedom fighters, left in heaps in Hungary to decay,
while old men rubbed against my thighs
lulling me to them with the hum,
Succumb, succumb.

Why couldn't I? When the world lapsed wide
and elastic into too much, too bright space when Kennedy died
and the road wore bald; and the yards stretched
between houses, the towns gleamed like chrome, I drove
into walls, day after day,
and the police shrugged like uncles, Obey, Obey.

Can't you bleed? Coward, can't you die
while wrists are cut, throats slit, children gassed
in Vietnam? At twenty-four can you only cry
while men shoot themselves to death in the DMZ
and your analyst coughs, You must, Christopher,
adjust, adjust.

Two of Your Great-Aunt's Dreams

You have found two of your great-aunt's dreams
spelled perfectly.

Each word the same space apart,
letters lined up
like young girls in seminary
trained to curtsy, to smooth their skirts over their laps,
to recite their Latin.

Sentences
like winding stairs in finishing schools,
leaded windows, dark wood
of very old houses. Paragraphs like high-ceilinged
dormitories, each letter arriving, cap in hand
like a pre-former,
or saying prayers the first night
as if she were being put to bed in a cathedral.

In one dream it is 1887,
this will be your aunt's first ride on a locomotive,
they are nearing the end of a tunnel:
"It was as if we were spiraling through a telescope
into the brilliant vistas of another,
magnified world. Of a sudden there was such a shrieking
lifting from nowhere
like flocks of startled, trapped birds
fluttering along the glass. We could smell feathers
and blood."

This sentence is written and crossed out thrice
as if she tried to rip out the shrieks
like stitches, to mend her dream.

"Every child looked for the screams
as if each were a different kind of cruel bird
whose talons were intended
for only one particular child. We curled around the talons
as if we had already been seized.
Even Papa cringed."

Your great-aunt writes how she reached the town
where she was to live forever.
We laugh and pretend this is a proper young girl's dream
of a wedding night she was never to have.

By seventeen she had brought two children into the world,
one stillborn.

In the second dream her father's voice grows faint,
he is wrapped in shawls upstairs.
She brings her friends up to say goodbye
as if it were they who were leaving.

In one of her letters she saved and sealed again
(you have to break off the old wax)
we find her father shot her mother
trying to wrest the gun from her breast
where she waved it like a fan.
She recalls the blood on her father's ruffled cuffs
where he broke the window to cry for help.

An old relative writes on a card with tiny flowers
she sends by servant:
> My Beloved Niece,
> Courage.

Each word is austere, graceful
as if it had been skated on ice,
each letter latches on to the next like child performers
in an ice capades, clasping the waist
of the one before,

The lithe and letter-perfect capitals gliding backwards
spinning away, sprinting back
like figure skaters

The loops and bows to each vowel,
the flourish to final letters,
ice lifting off their blades.

Jessie Vaughan

Brought South like a sideshow freak,
Indian princess, class valedictorian,
hoodwinked, breathing through the sill of the closet
where Dr. Ross locked you while he went after his gun,
forsaken for four other wives and President McKinley's daughter,
you short-order cooked and played the numbers
till the last thing that Indian giver gave you, long shot,
gambling debt, a son paid off.

The Black Sox hit the headlines
and you beat it back to Florida, shifting grandstands —
one day the hounds, the next the horses —
getting stiff on Cuba libres, postcarding advice to batters in slumps,
putting the twenties to bed like spoiled children,
the thirties, silent children
who had to learn to feed themselves. You lost your breasts
under another damn paleface's knife.

After the war you put your son's medals away
between his football jerseys,
put them away like winter clothes.
I was another of my mother's accidents. Ted Williams hit .406
and Ernestine Byer who had once sung with Caruso
brought you home with her
like a Filene's Basement bargain. Every April you'd drive her Caddy
from Cape Cod to Sarasota

Without backing up (you never learned reverse)
to catch spring training,

play the dogs, and ask the future of a talking horse
you knew in Georgia.
The seasons ground their gears,
you shifted sports, returning every year for opening day.
At eighty-three you came to cook for us
with two new dresses and a portable TV, like a high-school bride.

I grew up, tried to junk my car in the sea,
didn't take enough pills,
abandoned you in bed with tenpins, quiz shows, and incurable
        cancer;
at Ravenscraig ladies hid under their covers
as you cursed, "Nigger, you nigger,
throw that damn ball," as they walked the Kid once more,
forcing another run in.
I remember you listening for last night's scores in our kitchen

Stirring marmalade pudding,
telling me how your father used to say, "Jessie Vaughan,
piss or get off the pot."
We scatter your ashes into the surf off Cunningham's Bridge;
they flicker down like ticket stubs.
Nigger hater, spoilsport, sweet fanatic, my craziest fan,
old squaw,
you said you would dance at my wedding.

Dib

With pockets full of golf balls and butts
we'd saved from under porch rockers,
we watched her from the woods come in under par,
a woman women liked to say walked like a man.
We'd tease and say your mother walked like a guard in a women's
    prison,
striding from green to green, locking them up
with a great hoop of keys.

Poor Dib, our mothers liked to say, wandering into other houses
in her nightgown, smelling of cigarettes and cat hair.
When we saw her, we let our teasing die away. We caught back
    our serves.
Like a figure in a painting she rose over the hill
out of reach of any human sound;
we watched, half waving, rapt and still like details
painted into the background.

All day we charged food to our fathers, traded their dirty books
whose pages we remember still like the addresses
of old girls. We were too bored for singles, too old for war,
we strummed our racquets like back-up musicians.
Our mothers liked to talk of a car
or a house Dib had left burning. But she drove off the ladies' tee
as steady as our fathers and as far.

Timothy Proudfoot she named you, fat and slow,
the millionaire's son helping out behind the counter
of the paper store, or bringing buttered steaks to her,

listening, letting her atone.
We lay in the woods behind the 17th,
lighting up, getting hard-ons, dreaming of owning a car,
watching our mothers struggle in way over par.

I never knew Dib drank
till I knew my father did; he died of it.
How did they manage to put so much away,
rising drunk at meetings, trying to walk down the wings
of children's hospitals, blind wards
they had raised millions for,
telling the same old jokes on the Jews day after day?

Later tiring at the wheel, letting a carful of children sway
across the road, I think of my life as a child
as this: they in the front seat,
us in the back — they push their feet to the floor, hitting seventy,
eighty, they want to open the door
and step out into the mist
rising to the waist

As it sometimes does over golf courses long after
everyone has gone home, winds
hushed like galleries. Not one floodlight, not a star,
the last green left somewhere in the mist like a stalled car
and Dib is out there, practicing, practicing blind,
she is out there coming in under par.

Companions

She should have lived with silent, implacable women,
with cooks and housekeepers,
schoolfriends in salt-and-pepper tweed,
women whose second husbands had died leaving huge childless
    houses
with rooms named like children,
rooms kept ready, filled with dried flowers and historical novels.

Alice Edwards, Miriam Waterman,
Dottie Teale, Lucy Enright: women whose names sound
like chaste heroines of 1890
in New England romances where virtue triumphs over Jews
and oily anarchists; settlement girls
poets said had throats pale and lovely as a swan's.

She should have lived with women who had done with sex,
women gardening long after
the dark performed its marriages, body after body put away
like Books of Common Prayer,
women working down narrow gardens they plant by fences,
rooting musk and moss roses, beach heather and plum.

Who belly under barbed wire to bring back the first forsythia,
follow Near Eastern women on dark beaches,
mimic their lilt, show off for nieces,
who hum as they ride bicycles with fat tires and straw baskets
and dry rose petals on screens over furnaces
and sew them into sleeves.

Elderly women who sleep in boys' pajamas,
who read long novels of courtesans searching ruins
for their masters, old sorry tyrants
who straddled them weeping
like drunken fathers
who left them bewildered, made formal by an abiding love.

Women who read late and rise early
and pride themselves on their spelling, calling words in
from other rooms, who know the names for things:
gemstones, fossil rock, pottery, ships' knots, snakes;
who speak of men without bitterness,
owners of the rented houses they had lived in as girls.

"Yellow Is the Central Principle

of the nervous system as well as the exciting
principle of the brain; with a little red, it
is a cerebral stimulant. . . ."
                    — *Joseph Pancoast, 1876*

In Germany, yellow turnips, gold coins, saffron.
In England, yellow spiders rolled in butter for jaundice.
In Malaya the plague is driven away in a yellow ship.
Bits of gold are sprinkled on food in Greece;
the afflicted drink wine in which a gold piece has been left
for three nights exposed to the stars.

Ravens' eggs rubbed into old men's hair (the pouches
of cheeks filled with oil so their teeth
will not turn black), black threads for earache, black snails
rubbed on warts, skins of black animals
applied warm to palsied limbs,
black fowl, if buried where caught, to cure epilepsy.

In jaundice, if urine becomes a deeper red
until nearly black, if stains on linen cannot be removed,
it is a good sign; cover the sick with red,
wrap the feverish in red flannel. The breath of a red ox
soothes the convulsed. When the infirm awake
cloak yourself and come to them in crimson.

Pancoast with cabinets of color, Babbitt with colored panes
funneled light onto afflicted parts;
blue light for hemorrhages, yellow light for liver
and brain, deep yellows for impotency. In case of near death
notify these silent doctors of color,
then close relatives, then the usual physicians and priests.

Say the names of colors as if they were home remedies
and spells as if they should make you well.
I wish these words were colors,
gifts I had already wrapped, new clothes I was bringing you
to try on, stories we looked forward
to telling each other again.

Old woman, you would be scolding me now,
saying, "No, look closer, much closer, soften these solid colors,
make the light shine through them:
iron buff, stone yellow, seed pearl, old ivory.
Place only those colors next to each other
that help each other."

Kenny Brown

As a child I used to lie in bed whispering
"I like Negroes, I like Negroes"
in case one were about to climb in the window
and I could tell him I was just saying nice things about him
or about robbers
or perverts I imagined already in the house
sallow and bald, dressed in brown gabardine
like German spies. "Weary, weary," you show me
the two bandaged fingers you broke
on some white boy's jaw.
"No one pushes Kenny Brown around."

You wipe a shine into the rims
of the officers' coffee cups. You like this place
because you can lock it,
anyone in jail with a key has a certain dignity.
Afternoons, you sit on a folding chair beside the bookkeepers
and sweet-talk them
as you would a girlfriend's mother.
You are suing the county for $125,000,
you have learned grammar in jail: verb endings, possessives,
plurals. "Yessir, the mind
is a strange and wondrous creation."

I imagine you carrying your black bag
like a priest into houses.
What confessions
the suburbs must have blurted out to you.
When you are tired, I remember how young you are,

how you are in jail for forgetting
to throw away the gun you used
on your last all-night food market.
The prison smells like a factory
everyone has gone home from.

It's Good Friday,
in the hole a white boy is setting his bedding on fire.
He growls in the back of his throat,
lopes back and forth
like a feral child bayed at last.
All night the guards listen to his nails.

Kenny Brown knows better than to loop a belt around his neck.
He would have known better
than to leave such a boy his belt.

Oil Man

This is the room he keeps his bottles in.
It is like his dashboard where there is a wrench, screws
(threads stripped), shoelaces (two dozen, all colors), six wallet photos
of his married daughter when she was four and fat
and he used to bring home sacks of potatoes, the handle of a pail,
a pearl child's ring, pink stones from Plum Island Beach,
December from a desk calendar, two pages
from a thirteen-year-old's diary, a crucifix just out of reach.

All day he has been mowing grass, his boss Jimmy the Bookie's.
Now he is lying across his bed in boxer shorts
reading *Island of Desire*; soon he will have to shave and dress,
another friend's friend is dead. When I pass his room
all I see are pillboxes balanced one
on the edge of the other like children's letter blocks,
antacids, antihistamines, cough syrups, hair groom.

This is not a poem about raccoon coats, tuxedos
shedding like old cats, wide Florida ties
with naked ladies, or the tiny flowered dresses
Thelma Grassi gave him when her daughter took a fit
and smothered her baby. Everyone gives him things:
the button-down shirts and good shoes of the dead.
They call and he comes, he puts their clothes away.
He makes everything pay

But his oil truck. This poem is not about the nights at the door
of the room where his wife slept with his daughter,
how he waited like a sick child to be led back to bed.

This is not about those nights in bathrooms
afraid his stomach would bleed,
porcelain of the toilet cooling his brow, the severed heads and
        children
tied to radiators he makes himself read about and reread.

"Watch out for the Puerto Ricans, they like knives. The niggers,
they like the blade." He curls his fingers
as if there were razors between them,
he sips a little cherry brandy to soothe his supper,
bets his granddaughters' ages, picks up kings and keeps them.
He knows everyone: who brings trouble, who brings
the law. Saturdays he watches the club's door and goes for things.

All week he cleans out other people's cellars: old doors with holes
where the knobs were, laps with no cords, hand massagers,
Mixmasters, anything he can't fix and the tools
to fix it with, box full of tie boxes, box of used tubes
of denture cream, box of Popsicle sticks, face
of a clock, head of a china dog, postcards from the Vatican.
This cannot be a poem about everything he has to save
and hopes to sell: the flower baskets nailed out of split logs and
        twigs
he recovers in the rain off grave after grave.

Children of the Water

You wait for your brother to tease you,
to fling off your bedclothes and hold a gun to your head again.
At eight you were thrown from brother to brother,
slung over their shoulders,
buried in mock ceremonies under water.

Young and blond, you end every poem crushed into a fine powder.
You laugh how you will call your first book *Erosions,*
want nothing more than to dissolve,
disappear into the cuticles of leaves, be shade, be riverbed
sandpebbles sticking to the bottoms of boys' feet.

You tell me how in the Maori legend
Tane, god of trees, and Raumi, god of plants, tried to sever
their mother the sky from their father earth,
how Tu, god of beasts, pierced and shredded white membranes,
how Tane finally put his shoulders between

And thrust father and mother apart, this breathing space
I strain to keep
as if I had to think hard to stop us all from being crushed,
to keep our dimensions from caving in
like a mine shaft we had wandered into.

David, to love another man
I have to paste on metaphors, wings fastened with candle wax,
and edge out along the sills,
my body like a poorly made kite refusing to lift,
an eel strangling on its line.

I want to believe the myths you make me learn:
water rising, first man
and first woman climbing reed trees from other worlds,
yellow hawk and heron leading the other animals,
spiders spinning through cracks in each dome's shell.

First man and first woman fleeing, world after world,
the water rising, swaying
like a bear searching for her lost cubs;
nothing else matters but the space she must fill to the edges,
rearing, another shell cracking

Water lumbering into another age
batting civilizations aside like frightened campers,
raging for her cubs,
the children of the water
whom the coyote stole.

You are leaving,
your father tells you to screw with your boots on.
For the first time you tell me how afraid
you are to leave your brother in his room, four years
after the accident, one brother under another's wheels.

Three weeks ago lightning ran through your body
into his, making his eyes tear and blur
as he reached for you, thinking you had disappeared into the light,
screaming, "David, David," long after
the thunder's talons had loosened, releasing his voice.

As you tell me, your small, wiry hands clutch your feet
as they did then, trying to stop the pain
from passing out of your body.
You do not need this poem
stealing your beauty, your bravado

As the coyote stole the children of the water.
But I need to make you beautiful in my poem,
to place, as the Navajos recount,
the children of the water in a small boat
on a high and serene lake.

At the Mouth of the Cave

as if you were only taking short flights from these nesting places

You are close enough to death
to know its warm, dark temperatures.
It is like camping in a cave,
learning to sleep on the loose grit of old stone,
to watch bats blur and blow past, blind
and goatfooted as leaves,
scuttling like leaves, blind wings,
sly tongues that lap and suck,
scoop and nibble,
children making small treats last.

Being close to death you know little
that sings at a human pitch.
Death sings to you like radar,
you know its signals,
you are already sending the tiny bat shrills
of your brain into the dark: coding,
decoding. When you wake out of your coma
you remember your mother's songs
as if close to death she too had learned
its high continuous pitch.

She makes songs out of the pacts she swears you to,
lifting your limp hands: "Who dies first
shall wait at whatever crossroads may be.
Wait, my mouse-eared bat,
my little pipistrelle." When you wake
you remember waves of sound

the humming of caves
in which you hide deeper and deeper
making her find you, each time
closer to death.

In the trache ward, dozens of gray children
flutter like small bats.
Your mother cuts your name in the metal necklace
that covers the hole in your neck.
You touch your wheelchair and laugh, you miss your wings,
you say. We have to fold
and unfold them around you,
they dwarf you, Wendy;
touching you is like touching between the wings
the bat's soft brown fur.

Close to death, you crouch as if you were crawling
deeper into a cave;
your organs grow stunted and blind as fossil reptiles.
You have adapted to this sleep
as if you had been born in its crevices:
at its mouth you flicker and swerve
like those pipsqueak bats that sip pollens
crisscrossing openings, skiffs
tacking harbors
before they can sail free.

Roost here,
live always at the mouth of this cave.

Namesake

Christopher, fatherless, makeshift child,
little apostrophe hung like a cap
over an empty chair,
learn to make do with names only, households of gathered names,
names of wildflowers, their kitchen sounds,
butter-and-eggs, bedstraw, partridge peas,
may apple, bee balm,
milkwort, inkberry, innocence,
names cluttered like kitchens warm and steamy from use;
black under kitchen porcelain, taste of apple
and brown sugar on wooden spoons,
coffee and flour smells of cookbooks,
smells of dishtowels drying,
stone steps just scrubbed, warmth of gloves
taken off radiators,
stones warmed and laid under covers; imported ales
of early afternoon, last daylight
watered down like local beer,
nights like homemade blackberry cordials
your uncles let you stay up and sip,
that you tasted on your lips all next day;
bouquets just the names of colors give off, names
used like cooking wines or Near Eastern spices
till they are everyday: saffron, ivory, turquoise,
cochineal, jasper, mauve, indigo,
amethyst, amber. Christopher, one day
all our families will vanish — great ships built hurriedly, poorly,
arks, old farmhouses floating away from their farms.
We shall remember the dark smell of wood

that is always wet; damp resin
of bathhouses, must of rope, dories bottoms-up in boathouses
like cubs, cabin cruisers beside them
hibernating like old dams. We shall remember the scents
names mark their territories with
like bears. We shall remember
the names of other children on our desks,
inside schoolbooks, names
of characters our mothers made up stories about,
of boys they had crushes on in high school
(Chick Carbone, Bobby Duggan, Howie Reid)
uncles we've never met, aunts who smelled of lilac
and Yardley's lavender, names we remember
like the feel of a grownup's pocket: lint, crease dirt, crumbs,
keys, matches, loose change
we were allowed to count out and keep.

Bedtime

Nora pretends, eyes held shut,
thinking the voices of her dolls
until her lips move.
Christian asks if I will walk him to his stop;
the girls there tease and call him Small Bear.
When I remember to kiss him tonight
he holds still as if I am dressing a wound on his scalp.
I feel the hardness of his forehead on my lips all evening.
I lie in bed careful not to touch,
not to be touched.

I try to imagine this house drained of me,
my children's lives without me
like stiff, wet winter clothes
softening as they are put on again,
this world without me, only the half-moon,
the watermark where a glass was.
I write this because I am afraid.
I hear the pauses in breathing,
the dropped stitches,
the faint moans of my children
as they are sewn into their dreams.

Infidelities

When he has tired of loving his sons,
he breaks their microscopes and violins,
takes tablesilver out of their hands and bends the blades
till they snap. The boys stand closer to each other,
watch him plunge his hands
through starbursts of broken glass.

They feel the cool inside their shirts,
rub threads in their pockets,
try to remember the secret powers
they choose up at recess: who can melt,
who can be invisible first.

He clutches the oldest,
presses his thumbs into the boy's shoulders,
twists him like a wick.
His angers are clear as hot wax,
they cloud and harden.
The other children sing nervously, study their nails,
bite loose skin off their lips.

In the evening he sweeps up the glass in his children's room,
first the broken petals,
wrists of glass, emptied faces; then the slivers,
fingernails, filaments,
a fine dust of glass he leaves between the floorboards.
He moves quietly around his sleeping children,
touches one's bare heel, one's hard fist.

From These Hands Nothing

For a moment today I was tired enough to believe
I could ease your sorrow,
we would lie in a green dark listening to the shades,
knowing if we lifted ourselves
we could have the light again,
could watch the children darken like stones
the sea glazes and glides back.

Knowing nothing will change because we wish it so,
we grow heavy, clumsy in each other's arms;
aching to speak, we dare not speak.
From these hands nothing shall flow.

I herd pills across the table,
take a shepherd's comfort in this flock's indifference.
"I will be better," you weep softly.
I pace holding my chest
as if all the parts of my body might spill
like beads off an unraveling string toy.

Knowing nothing changes because we wish it so,
I do not grow gentler, more resourceful;
in anguish I only move more slowly.
From these hands nothing shall flow.

In spite of days when I return to morning service in your arms,
practicing an old faith,
our bodies rocking back and forth like true believers,
I peel your body off me, that old temptation,

I keep true to my painted ladies,
my sisters of the night: grief, regret, remorse,
sweet sluts easily satisfied.

Trees nod their huge animal heads at our windows,
blown sideways, rubbing shanks,
branches bowing their long strenuous necks,
livestock grazing in a final wind,
hobbled to old hungers, knowing nothing shall change
because they wish it so.
From these hands nothing shall flow.

Gravity

Although I push little Nora off the roof,
edge over to see her clear,
bounce, and shatter like our best wedding china,
nothing ever breaks here,
I can't even sin,
Nora's back on the eaves, butt complacent as a nest:
gravity can't seem to win.

Although I tear up that false sentiment, a son,
conceit I can't sustain, each simile,
fine phrase, each shred of every sound
is gathered in midair,
Christian's back, elastic and indispensable
as underwear:
nothing here hits the ground.

Although I let my parents be washed away
like a summer home,
insurance I try to collect, deadweight
I try to jettison,
abandoned on ice they learn to skate, in nursing homes
they bob upright and float:
no one anymore goes down with the boat.

Although I bury my wife, pipes swelling,
no one will buy this place;
just when at last I think I'm rid of her,

closing the sale,
all my old loves adjust
like ghosts
and rise telltale.

Making Camp in an Empty Park

Water moccasin, wood thrush, field mouse —
when the sounds lose their names, branch by branch,
and the cars are eased away
like children from swings
and we turn our backs to the fire,
old relative at whose dying bedside we have watched,
and our girl, then our boy
are stolen and fondled, bodies yielding like farm animals,
when there is nothing left
but the woods hunched on its forelegs,
wings tucked under,
flies circling its foul rump,
when after a great reluctance even you let go my hand

Il Duce, Spring, Little Papa

Foxglove, fevercup, hawkweed, bindweed, loosestrife,
poor Robin's plantain, moth mullein, pennyroyal,
jack-in-the-pulpit, nightshade, lucky lady:
secret code my mother made me learn
as if there were time for nothing else.
In some border town the truce is broken,
seeds wake, flung
like boys from skidding cars.
From remote hills I watch my mother taken again
by madness, that grand confederacy.
I want to dash back, be dragged away with her
like a bright-eyed patriot.
Seasons change, stinking of their cheap wines,
vines climb each others' shoulders
like crowds in a newsreel hurrahing Il Duce, Spring, Little Papa,
fat dictator on his balcony.
I want to climb a water tower,
draw a bead.
Hate presses his soft boy's mouth on mine,
roots soak in their baths.
Nothing comes naturally to me.
When I was six, I skinned off forsythia
and whipped myself with green shoots, imagining men
making me betray her.
My sons romp below like city dogs unleashed,
they bail out of trees,
fold in my arms like parachutes.
Another spring we shall come back
to watch the flowers break surface like drowning girls.

Town Beach

You liked to swim out over your head, pretend to drown,
only your feet out of water, plucked white roots.
Convinced, I curved my body around me,
shoulders rounded, tightening
as if trying to pull the ends of a bow together.

You curved my hand around tillers,
held it there, taught me to steer our Herreshoff through jetties,
that wide white house being moved.
I want you to put your hands under me again,
teach me the dead man's float.

I think of you at nine, growing furiously
more beautiful, more adamant
like a shell,
a lady's ear, a Chinese alphabet.

I wanted us only to test the water,
early mornings carrying blankets down from the bathhouse,
to make war before anyone else,
bunker in the deep shade under the lifeguard's boat,
dab blood off our feet from broken bottles in the dunes,
feel the beach slowly taken back from us,
unwrap wax paper from sandwiches softened by the sun,
tie towels around our waists
and let our bathing suits drop like parts of bodies
we could not use anymore,
each spanking his own bottom cool and soft as the sand
under the bathhouse.

When they put mother away,
you beat your head against the playroom wall,
pulling out of aunts' arms,
pulling back to the wall
with the steadfast, magnetic fury
of dogs hurling themselves against locked cellar doors.

I want your ruins back, the spiraling staircases of sand,
vestibules and corridors, turrets and eaves,
friezes you chiseled under cornices,
columns you weakened,
foundations you made me mold out of wet sand,
then shaved.

I want the slowly emptied cuffs and sleeves of long afternoons
to crawl back into the cold white sand
under the bathhouse and listen to showers
gasp and drowse like old men sleeping in the sun,
water seeping and filling the spaces between floorboards;
to lie under men's rooms
and smell their dark politics, listen to sounds of bathing suits
being squeezed through wringers,
to be four again and afraid to touch the rollers,
crying out, "No, no. Don't!"
as you let your hand ride up them;
to lie with you on late afternoons and look up through floorboards,
needing only slants of light
and skin to imagine women dressing above us,
to listen to them whisper
like voices from the future.

Standing Watch

"Don't you love to watch people?" the girl asks,
already bored with faces
like the dirty mouths and cheeks of dolls
and with you and your hands.
She lets you bend her this way and that;
you remember holding other children's dolls —
no matter where you touched, they were stiff and hollow.

You go out with girls so you have that part of your life
accounted for — it is like having a phone
so you won't have to explain why you don't.
You played with other children
so your father would suspect nothing,
you played your own games in and out of theirs.

You say nothing but speak to others so often in your mind
you wonder afterwards why they do not remember.
You touch your lips to feel if you have spoken.

Teachers called you sensitive; children sissy, mossface —
they said it grew on your teeth.
Your father burned your dolls.
The soft rubber melted off their faces.
Now you hold tight to books as if they too might be seized back.

If you stare into strangers' faces too long, too often,
you will exhaust their indifference.

When it is too late to speak, you remember entire speeches,
as a child lost remembers clearings,
every step into the wilderness but the last few.

You loved forsythia for the darkness inside,
branches for the spaces under them.
You watched places because the minute you didn't
people disappeared.

At four you would sit your dolls inside the forsythia
and watch the house all day.
If you stood watch long enough she would return,
you would go home and find
she had never left. Now you watch windows and doors
for the same reasons you read books:
to keep people from leaving by them.

When Are You Going to Grow Up?

My sons bring me skulls from the water company's woods,
spiders, dead bats, lizards,
old murder weapons in cases still not solved.
My oldest boy wants to know if we are returning
to the age of dinosaurs,
afraid of the monsters they are dredging lakes for
like stolen cars. My three-year-old lies on museum floors,
"You can't touch me, I am dead."
Death gives him power over us.

I still cannot name the things I was afraid of as a child:
the three black plants
beside the sunken garbage pail that was only an excuse
to cover the hole
that went straight to the middle of the earth.

Three ugly plants
like words spelled so badly you can't look them up,
black whiskers knotted like bibs
around the chins of pirates who clambered up our wall,
boarded our becalmed house every night.

Three stiff beards,
three silent uncles lifted out of the ground by their chins,
three tramps always at our kitchen door.
I remember an old man
chalking our gate, grabbing my brother and me,
shaking us, "Your mother's vicious crazy, boys!"
while mother shrieked from the porch.

I was sure there was a hole
that went straight down to the middle of the earth.
I could never see the bottom.
I used to lift the pail in and out of the dark
or rush out, push open the lid with my foot, and run.
I loved to hear the iron rim ring behind me.

Mother tried to show me there was a bottom to everything,
an end I could touch if I reached far enough.
She tried to make me touch everything I feared:
these three nameless plants outside our kitchen door, dead rodents,
old muskrats that would not decompose.
I would not touch a thing.

Power Man

for Justin once more in coma

Today you are power man
and the birds stun you
and I have to lift you onto the daybed in the attic
and press old spoons into your cheeks

Or place warm pennies on your forehead,
stroke a gull's feather over the folds of skin
between your fingers,
close your hands around a stone,
one of those dark with dirt we like best,
the kind we keep burying with our hands
and finding again.
I touch a bird's bones to your lips.

I lift your eyelids and stare into the dark hole,
that tunnel you tell me
you crawl in and out of while we sleep.
"I can climb in and out of my brains, Daddy."

You lie still
as if you were learning to float.

I am courage man, this afternoon,
carry you home to powders and potions,
draw your sisters' souvenir scarfs over your eyes,
hold pocket mirrors to your lips,
curl your fingers around my grandfather's smudged chess pieces.
I make your fingers find their fake bottoms
where the antidote lies.

The tips of your fingers press back
against mine, once more you have tired of holding your breath,
of playing dead. "No, wounded,"
you say, knowing I won't play dead with anyone.
"When you were a little boy, Daddy,
I was your friend and we climbed Nana's rocks
and threw stones at gulls.
Once I hit one."